Strange Ways to Earn a Living

By Stephen Rickard

Published in 2026 by
Norwood House Press
2544 Clinton Street
Buffalo, NY 14224

Printed in the United States of America

Library of Congress Cataloging-in-Publication Data:
Names: Rickard, Stephen, 1957-, author. | Hawkins, Daisy, author. | Gibbeson, Sara, illustrator.
Title: Strange ways to earn a living / by Stephen Rickard. The ticket / written by Daisy Hawkins, illustrated by Sara Gibbeson
Description: Buffalo, NY : Norwood House Press, 2026. | Series: Phonics all-stars: phase 5c
Identifiers: ISBN 9781978578623 (pbk.) | ISBN 9781978578630 (library bound) | ISBN 9781978578647 (ebook)
Subjects: LCSH: Reading–Phonetic method–Juvenile literature. | English language–Phonetics–Juvenile literature. | Occupations–Juvenile literature. | Vocational guidance–Juvenile literature. | Snowboarding–Juvenile fiction.
Classification: LCC LB1573.3 R534 2026 | DDC 372.465–dc23

CPSIA compliance information: Batch #CW26NHP: For further information contact Norwood House Press at 1-800-237-9932.

Some adults have quite boring jobs.

For example, would you like to be a sentry outside a royal residence? There'd be so much standing around.

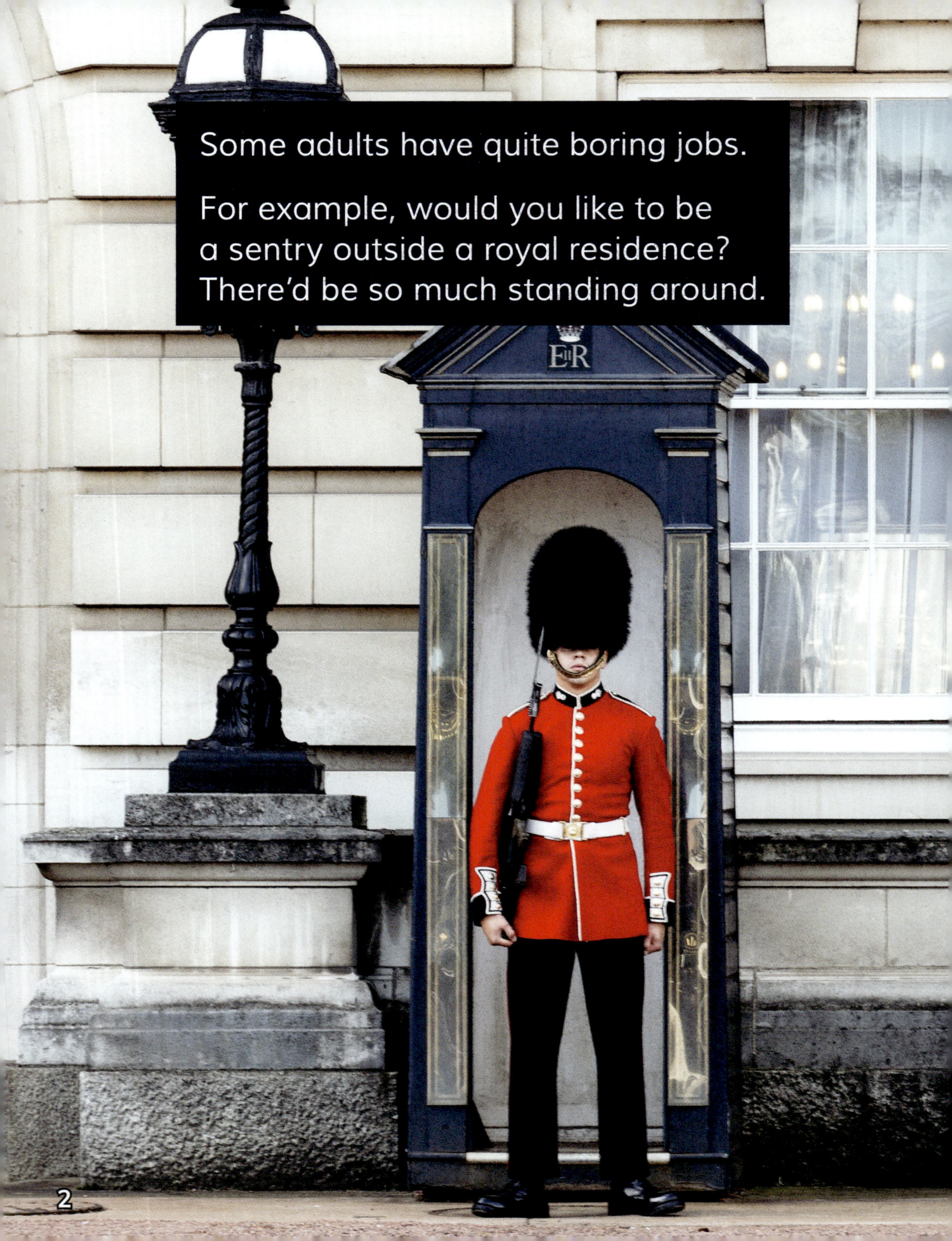

On the other hand, some people have quite interesting jobs. Do you think being a zookeeper would be fun?

Have you ever thought about some of the strangest jobs you could have?

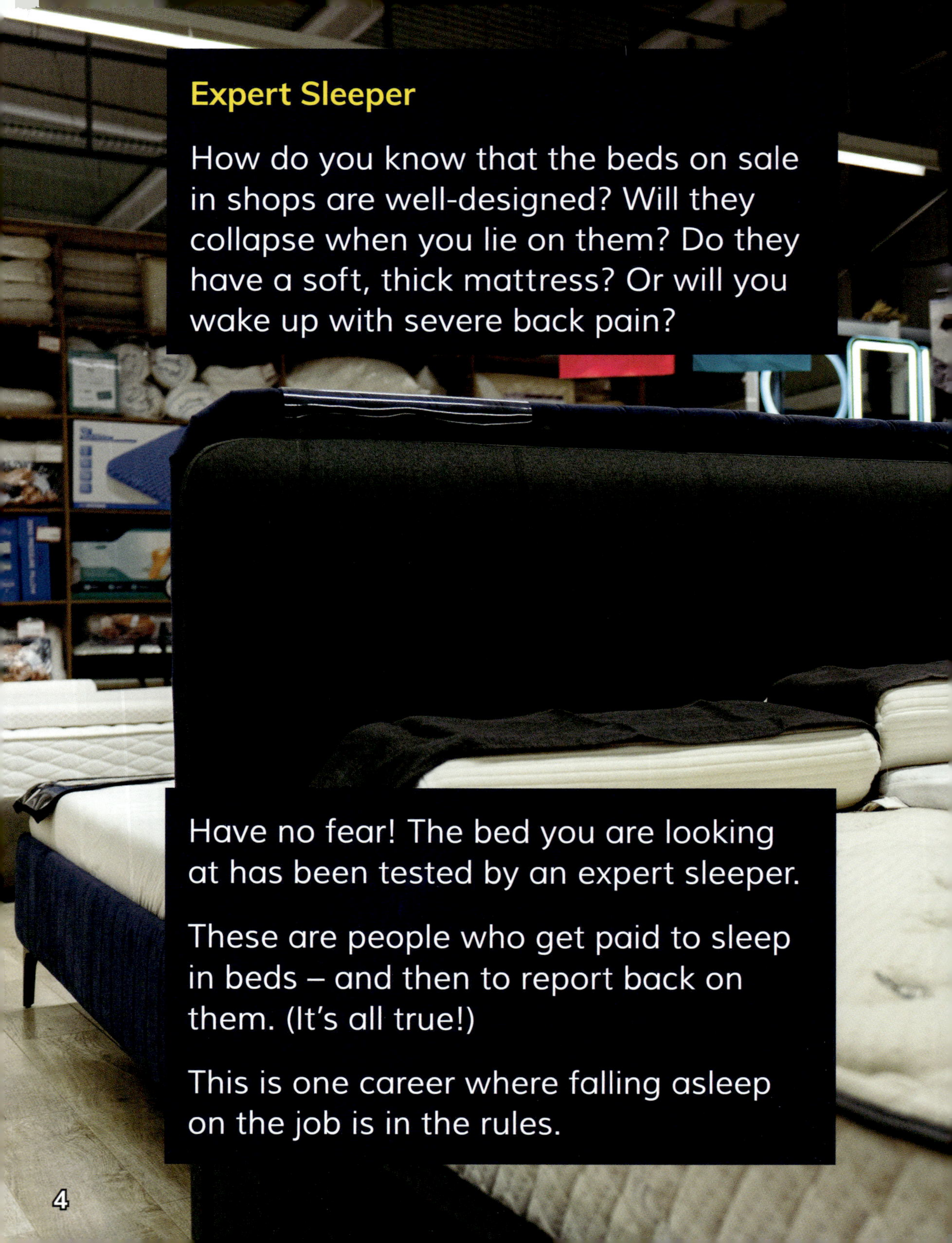

Expert Sleeper

How do you know that the beds on sale in shops are well-designed? Will they collapse when you lie on them? Do they have a soft, thick mattress? Or will you wake up with severe back pain?

Have no fear! The bed you are looking at has been tested by an expert sleeper.

These are people who get paid to sleep in beds – and then to report back on them. (It's all true!)

This is one career where falling asleep on the job is in the rules.

-25%
-20%

Product Sniffer

Imagine purchasing a car that smells of fish, or face cream that smells as if a wet dog has chewed it. Who would want that?

A product sniffer's job is to check that, when new products are sold, they don't smell terrible.

Water Slide Tester

Somebody needs to check that water slides in hotels and theme parks are safe – and fun!

Nobody wants to get injured on a water slide, but at the same time nobody wants it to be boring.

So a water slide tester's job is to check that the slide is safe and that it offers loads of enjoyment.

Pet Food Taster

People are happy to spend lots of money on food for their pets.

So pet food must look and smell wonderful to the people who pay for it and, for the pets who eat it, the taste must be excellent too.

Your job, as a pet food taster, is to check that the pet food looks good, smells good – and, yes, tastes good.

Teddy Bear Doctor

Have you seen those shops where little children can go in and make up a teddy bear of their own?

Well, each one of those shops has a repair person in the shop. Their only job is to mend injured teddy bears.

The teddy bear doctor might have to fasten arms or legs back on, and sometimes teddy bears need stitches, just like humans.

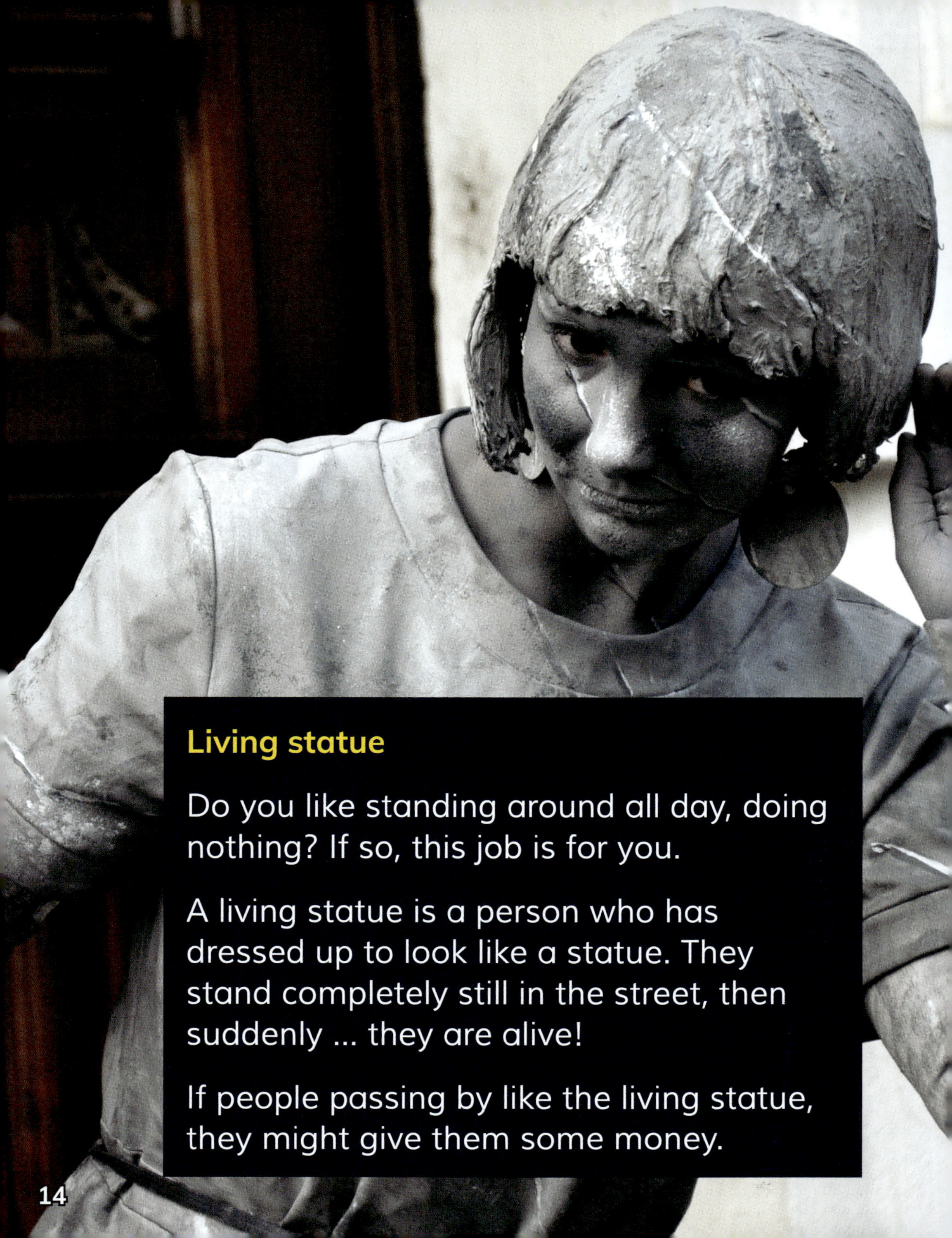

Living statue

Do you like standing around all day, doing nothing? If so, this job is for you.

A living statue is a person who has dressed up to look like a statue. They stand completely still in the street, then suddenly ... they are alive!

If people passing by like the living statue, they might give them some money.

If you can add some magic too, that is even better!

Snake milker

Some kinds of snakes produce venom with important chemicals in it. We can use these chemicals to cure diseases.

A snake milker's job is to "milk" the venom from the snakes and capture it, so that we can use it to treat people.

The Ticket

Written by
Daisy Hawkins

Illustrated by
Sara Gibbeson

Evert's eyes lit up at the sight of the mountain, towering over the rooftops.

"Come on, Evert!" Karl shouted.

His friends were waiting for him at the door of the music venue.

“Concert tonight, snowboarding tomorrow!” Evert grinned. “This is going to be a great vacation.”

Hurrying to his friends, Evert pulled out some cash to give to the man at the door.

The man handed him a bright red ticket.

"Keep this safe," he said. "If you go out for a bit, you cannot get back in without it."

Evert tucked the ticket into his wallet.

The next day, Evert and his friends were up the mountain in their snowsuits.

They had mastered all the marked runs.

"This is too easy," said Nils. "Let's head down that way."

Nils looked away from the resort slope, pointing to snow that was fresh and unspoiled.

Evert grinned. If the normal slopes were a thrill, this would be epic.

The boys pushed off.

Instantly it was much harder. Rocks jutted out of the snow and tree branches crossed their path.

After a while, there was a noise like thunder.

The boys looked around to see a mass of snow that had broken loose. As it slid downhill, it picked up speed – and gathered even more snow.

Horrified, Evert shifted his weight to speed up.

He could see Karl, not far from him, and Nils, further down the slope.

As he swerved to get close to Karl, Evert saw that it was now too late.

He tumbled head over heels, feeling the weight of cool snow all around him.

Then there was silence.

"Evert?"

Evert could hear panic in Karl's voice.

"Karl! Are you hurt?"

"No, just a bit bruised. But I am stuck under the snow."

"Me too. But it's OK. Nils was further ahead – he will have got away. He'll get help."

Time ticked on ...

What if Nils had not escaped the snow?

Evert pushed the thought away. He needed to think of a way to show the rescue team exactly where they were.

His right arm was squashed against his body, but he could lift it a bit ...

Was there something that might save them?

A bit later, Evert's ears pricked up at a faint noise.

Voices!

Nils must have got away! Now a rescue team was on the scene.

Quickly, Evert forced a hand up to the surface, clutching their one chance of being seen.

He stretched and stretched and stretched.

"We've got you, boys!" said a voice.

Evert felt a hand grab his own.

"You are so lucky you had this bright red ticket," said the voice. "We would never have spotted you without it."